Introduct

T0288638

Do you like the countryside or do you like cities? In the countryside, there are trees and fields. In cities, there are buildings, streets, and lots of people.

countryside

city

Do you live in a city?
What can you see in a city?
What can you do in a city?

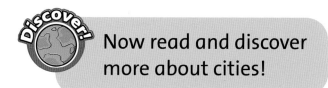

Now read and discover more about cities!

1 What Is a City?

It's seven o'clock in the morning.
People are going to work. It's a
new day in the city.

What is a city? A city is streets
and buildings. A city is cars,
buses, and taxis. A city is people –
lots of people.

Discover!

In some very big cities,
there are more than
15 million people!

Cities

Richard Northcott

Contents

OXFORD
UNIVERSITY PRESS

OXFORD
UNIVERSITY PRESS

Great Clarendon Street, Oxford, OX2 6DP, United Kingdom

Oxford University Press is a department of the University of Oxford. It furthers the University's objective of excellence in research, scholarship, and education by publishing worldwide. Oxford is a registered trade mark of Oxford University Press in the UK and in certain other countries

ISBN: 978 0 19 464682 6

An Audio Pack containing this book and an Audio download is also available, ISBN 978 0 19 402155 5

This book is also available as an e-Book, ISBN 978 0 19 410856 0.

An accompanying Activity Book is also available, ISBN 978 0 19 464672 7

Printed in China

This book is printed on paper from certified and well-managed sources.

ACKNOWLEDGEMENTS

Cover photograph: Alamy (Los Angeles aerial view/Chad Ehlers)

Illustrations by: Kelly Kennedy pp 4, 17; Dusan Pavlic/Beehive Illustration pp 20, 24, 26, 28, 32, 34, 38, 39; Alan Rowe pp 20, 22, 24, 26, 28, 30, 32, 34, 38, 39.

The Publishers would also like to thank the following for their kind permission to reproduce photographs and other copyright material: Alamy pp 3 (city/Yuen Man Cheung), 5 (city/Andy Selinger), 7 (Prisma by Dukas Pressagentur GmbH), 8 (Chad Ehlers), 9 (Christina Ferrin), 10 (Travelstock44), 11(boat/Travel Pictures), 12 (Imagebroker), 14 (cosmetics counter/Alex Segre), 15 (David Noton Photography), 16 (Neil Setchfield), 17 (J Marshall – Tribaleye Images); Getty Images pp 4 (EschCollection/The Image Bank), 6 (Buenos Aires/Henrik Dolle/Eye Em), 11 (rickshaws/Bloomberg), 13 (Art on File. Inc/Corbis Documentary), 14 (office/Mascot), 19 (Johannes Mann/The Image Bank); Oxford University Press pp 5 (map reading), 6 (viewing gallery), 17 (Underground/Shutterstock), 18 (Alamy); Shutterstock p. 3 (countryside/MN Studio).

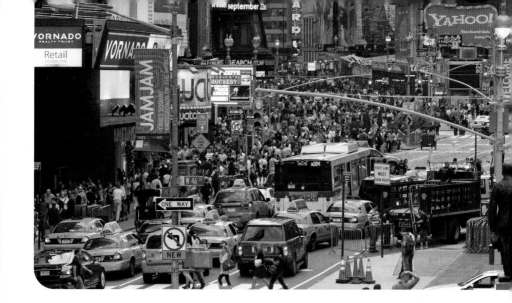

Now it's eleven o'clock. There are lots of people in the streets. People are going shopping. People are taking buses and taxis.

Some of the people are tourists. Every day, new people come to the city.

Tourists

→ Go to pages 20–21 for activities.

2 Buildings

In a city, you can see lots of buildings. There are museums, schools, and stores.

In some cities there are very tall buildings. Sometimes you can go to the top and look at the city.

The streets are for everyone. You can walk with your family or friends. You can look in store windows. You can watch people, cars, and buses.

A mall is a street with no cars. It's in a building, and you can find stores and restaurants there. There's a big, old mall in Milan in Italy. Tourists go to this mall and they take photos.

A Mall in Milan

→ Go to pages 22–23 for activities.

3 Water

Sydney

Many big cities are by an ocean. They have a harbor for ships. Ships bring materials for new buildings. Ships bring tourists, too.

There's a big harbor in Sydney in Australia. There are nice apartments and restaurants by the harbor. Sydney is a big city, but it has lots of parks and trees.

Ships can come to a city by river, too. Many cities are on big rivers. In these cities you can find great bridges. There are bridges for people, cars, and trains.

Discover!

Pittsburgh is a city in the USA. It has more than 400 bridges!

bridge

→ Go to pages 24–25 for activities.

4 Tourists

It's fun to be a tourist in a city.
There are lots of things to do. You
can go to a park, a museum, or a
zoo. You can ride on a bus and listen
to a guide.

It's good to walk around a city, too.
You can take photos of the streets
and buildings.

Udaipur

boat

In some cities there are lakes. You can swim there and have fun. In Udaipur in India, there's a big lake. You can ride in a boat on the lake.

In Hanoi in Vietnam, you can ride in a rickshaw and see the city.

Hanoi

rickshaw

Go to pages 26–27 for activities.

5 Homes

In cities, many homes are small. Some people live in houses, but many people live in apartments.

These apartments are in Berlin in Germany. They are nice apartments. Every apartment has a balcony. There's a playground for children, too.

Berlin

balcony

playground

stairs

San Francisco

These houses are in San Francisco in the USA. They have stairs and a balcony. There are trees and flowers in the street. These houses are 100 years old. Behind the houses there are big, new offices. San Francisco is an old city, but it has lots of new buildings.

→ Go to pages 28–29 for activities.

Work

In the morning, people come to cities and go to work. Lots of people work in offices. They use telephones and computers, but they don't meet many people at work.

Salesclerks meet lots of people at work. Salesclerks work in stores. They help us when we want to buy things.

In an Office

In a Store

salesclerk

Police Officers

Police officers meet lots of people, too. They help people in the city. They work in the day and at night.

There are doctors and nurses, teachers and students, bus drivers and taxi drivers. Thousands of people work together in a city.

→ Go to pages 30–31 for activities.

 # 7 Transportation

It's great to walk in a city, but you can't walk everywhere. Many people in cities use transportation.

Lots of people come to cities by car, so there are traffic jams. Cars make pollution. Cars are not a good type of transportation in big cities.

Trams are a good type of transportation. They run on tracks, and they don't make pollution.

tram

tracks

An Underground Station

Lots of cities have underground trains. Underground trains are fast. Thousands of people use them every day. Some underground stations are very deep.

One station in Kiev in Ukraine is 105 meters under the ground.

(105 meters)

 Go to pages 32–33 for activities.

8 Fun

In a Park

It's three o'clock in the afternoon. People are having fun in the park. They are riding in boats on the lake or talking to friends.

At seven o'clock in the evening, many people are at the theater or watching a movie. Maybe they are with their friends in a restaurant. In a city, there are lots of things to do in the evening.

It's twelve o'clock at night. Some people are in cafés and restaurants. Some people are working. Taxi drivers and police officers work at night. Many people are at home.

This is the end of our day in the city.

Go to pages 34–35 for activities.

1 What Is a City?

Read pages 4–5.

1 Write the words.

buildings   bus   people   ~~city~~   taxi   street

1 ___city___   2 _____   3 _____

4 _____   5 _____   6 _____

2 Circle the correct words.

1 People go to **work** / **tourists** in the morning.

2 In some **big** / **small** cities, there are more than 15 million people.

3 There are lots of tourists in **cities** / **people**.

4 Every day new **people** / **day** come to the city.

3 Complete the sentences.

buses   eleven   going
cities   ~~streets~~   taking

1 There are ___streets___ and buildings in a city.

2 There are cars and _____.

3 In _____ there are lots of people.

4 At _____ o'clock, there are lots of people in the streets.

5 People are _____ shopping.

6 People are _____ taxis and buses.

4 Order the words.

1 o'clock / It's / seven / in / morning. / the
___It's seven o'clock in the morning.___

2 are / going / work. / People / to
_____

3 It's / in / the / city. / a / new / day
_____

4 day / Every / people / come / the / city. / to
_____

② Buildings

← Read pages 6–7.

1 **Write the words. Then match.**

1 e t s o r

    store

2 m e m u s u

    _____

3 o c o s h l

    _____

4 l m a l

    _____

2 **Find and write the words.**

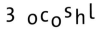 familyfriendswindowphotorestaurantpeople

1 _family_	3 _____	5 _____
2 _____	4 _____	6 _____

3 Circle the correct words.

1 A **mall** / **house** is a street with no cars.

2 There are **buses** / **stores** in a mall.

3 There are **restaurants** / **cars** in a mall, too.

4 There's a **mall** / **big** in Milan.

5 The mall in Milan is big and **new** / **old**.

6 Milan is a **countryside** / **city** in Italy.

4 Complete the sentences.

1 In cities there are _lots of buildings_ .
(buildings / lots / of)

2 There are museums, _____.
(schools, / and / stores)

3 In some cities there are _____.
(buildings / tall / very)

4 You can walk in the streets _____.
(with / family / your)

5 You can look _____.
(windows / in / store)

6 You can watch people, _____.
(and / cars, / buses)

3 Water

← Read pages 8–9.

1 Complete the puzzle.

2 Write *true* or *false*.

1 Sydney is in Italy. _false_

2 There's a harbor in Sydney. _____

3 Sydney is a small city. _____

4 There are parks in Sydney. _____

5 Pittsburgh is in the USA. _____

6 There aren't any bridges in Pittsburgh. _____

3 Complete the sentences.

big   buildings   come   ocean

1 Many cities are by an _____ .

2 Ships bring materials for new _____ .

3 Many cities are on _____ rivers.

4 Ships can _____ to a city by river.

4 Answer the questions.

1 Where is Sydney?

   It's in Australia.

2 Is Sydney by the ocean?

   _____

3 What is by the harbor in Sydney?

   _____

4 Where is Pittsburgh?

   _____

5 Is there a river in Pittsburgh?

   _____

6 How many bridges does Pittsburgh have?

   _____

(4) Tourists

← Read pages 10–11.

boat   guide
lake   park
rickshaw   tourists

1 Write the words.

1 _____   2 _____   3 _____

4 _____   5 _____   6 _____

2 Circle the correct words.

1 It's fun to be a **tourist** / **building** in a city.

2 There are **lots** / **parks** and museums.

3 You can listen to a **photo** / **guide**.

4 It's good to **walk** / **take** around a city.

5 In Udaipur you can **walk** / **ride** in a boat.

6 In Hanoi you can ride in a **rickshaw** / **family**.

3 Match.

1 There are lots of	in a boat.
2 You can	a big lake.
3 In Udaipur there's	in India.
4 You can ride on the lake	go to a museum.
5 Udaipur is a city	things to do in a city.

4 Order the words.

1 be / to / tourist. / a / It's / fun

_____

2 can / to / You / park. / go / a

_____

3 bus. / can / a / You / ride / on

_____

4 a / good / to / city. / It's / around / walk

_____

5 of / buildings. / take / photos / can / You

_____

⑤ Homes

← Read pages 12–13.

apartment   children
flowers   playground
house   tree

1 Write the words.

1 _____ 2 _____ 3 _____

4 _____ 5 _____ 6 _____

2 Circle the correct words.

1 Many homes in cities are **big** / **small**.

2 Many **buildings** / **people** in cities live in apartments.

3 Some apartments have **balconies** / **houses**.

4 There are **nice** / **street** apartments in Berlin.

5 **San Francisco** / **Berlin** is in the USA.

3 Complete the sentences.

offices   old   stairs   USA

1 San Francisco is in the _____ .

2 There are some _____ houses in
San Francisco.

3 Some houses in San Francisco have
_____ and a balcony.

4 Behind some houses in San Francisco
there are _____ .

4 Match. Then write the sentences.

Many homes in	an old city.
People live in	houses or apartments.
San Francisco is	Germany.
Berlin is in	cities are small.

1 _Many homes in cities are small._

2 _____

3 _____

4 _____

6 Work

← Read pages 14–15.

1 **Write the words. Then match.**

1 axit redvir

_____

2 pheelnote

_____

3 elcipo rfofeci

_____

4 mectroup

_____

2 **Find and write the words.**

morningsalesclerkstorenurseteacherthousand

1 _____   3 _____   5 _____

2 _____   4 _____   6 _____

3 Circle the correct words.

1 Lots of people in cities **make** / **work** in offices.

2 People in offices **use** / **meet** telephones and computers.

3 People in offices don't meet lots of **stores** / **people** at work.

4 Salesclerks meet lots of **people** / **computers**.

5 Salesclerks help people in **offices** / **stores**.

6 Police officers help **people** / **telephones** in the city.

4 Complete the sentences.

1 In the morning, _____ .
   (go / work / people / to)

2 Lots of people _____ .
   (in / offices / work)

3 Salesclerks _____ .
   (work / in / stores)

4 When we are in a store, _____ .
   (help / us / salesclerks)

5 Thousands of people _____ .
   (a / city / work / in)

7 Transportation

← Read pages 16–17.

1 Complete the puzzle.

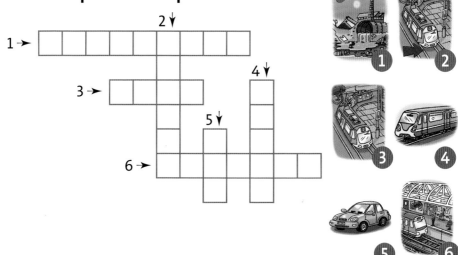

2 Write *true* or *false*.

1 In a city, you can walk everywhere. _____

2 Cars can be a problem in big cities. _____

3 Trams run on tracks. _____

4 Trams make lots of pollution. _____

5 Underground trains are fast. _____

6 There aren't any underground
   trains in Kiev. _____

3 Complete the sentences.

can't   cities   don't   car   station   Thousands

1 You _____ walk everywhere in the city.
2 Lots of people come to cities by _____, so there are traffic jams.
3 In some _____ there are trams.
4 Trams _____ make pollution.
5 _____ of people use underground trains everyday.
6 One underground _____ in Kiev is very deep.

4 Order the words.

1 to / walk / It's / great / city. / a / in

_____

2 transportation. / Many / people / use

_____

3 make / Cars / pollution.

_____

4 tracks. / on / run / Trams

_____

8 Fun

← Read pages 18–19.

park   restaurant
evening   theater
afternoon   movie

1 Write the words.

 1 _____

 2 _____

 3 _____

 4 _____

 5 _____

 6 _____

2 Write the times.

1 _It's three o'clock._

2 _____

3 _____

4 _____

3 Match.

1 It's fun to go to the park

2 Some parks

3 There are lots of things

4 People meet their

5 Some people

6 At twelve o'clock at night,

to do in the evening.

friends in restaurants.

many people are at home.

have a lake.

work at night.

in the afternoon.

4 Answer the questions.

1 Where do people go in the afternoon?

_____

2 What can you do in the park?

_____

3 Where do people go in the evening?

_____

4 Who works at night?

_____

A City Fact File

1 Think about your city or a city near you.

2 Write a fact file for the city.

What is the name
of the city? _____

Is it by an ocean?

_____

Is it on a river?

_____

What buildings are there?

_____

What transportation is there?

_____

What do people do to have fun?

_____

3 Make more city fact files.

A Cities Poster

1 Complete the charts about cities.

Cities by an Ocean

Sydney in Australia

_____

_____

_____

Cities on Big Rivers

_____

_____

_____

_____

Cities with Old Buildings

_____

_____

_____

_____

Cities with Underground Trains

_____

_____

_____

_____

2 Find or draw pictures of the cities.
Make a poster.

3 Display your poster.

Picture Dictionary

 apartment

 buildings

 buy

 children

 city

 countryside

 cross

 deep

 fast

 fields

 guide

 harbor

 lake

 mall

 materials

 million

museum ocean office photo

pollution river ship shopping

station street thousand top

tourists traffic jam transportation underground

Oxford Read and Discover

Series Editor: Hazel Geatches • CLIL Adviser: John Clegg

Oxford Read and Discover graded readers are at six levels, for students from age 6 and older. They cover many topics within three subject areas, and support English across the curriculum, or Content and Language Integrated Learning (CLIL).

Available for each reader:
• Audio Pack
• Activity Book

Available for selected readers:
• e-Books

Teaching notes & CLIL guidance: **www.oup.com/elt/teacher/readanddiscover**

Level / Subject Area	The World of Science & Technology	The Natural World	The World of Arts & Social Studies
1 — 300 headwords	• Eyes • Fruit • Trees • Wheels	• At the Beach • In the Sky • Wild Cats • Young Animals	• Art • Schools
2 — 450 headwords	• Electricity • Plastic • Sunny and Rainy • Your Body	• Camouflage • Earth • Farms • In the Mountains	• Cities • Jobs
3 — 600 headwords	• How We Make Products • Sound and Music • Super Structures • Your Five Senses	• Amazing Minibeasts • Animals in the Air • Life in Rainforests • Wonderful Water	• Festivals Around the World • Free Time Around the World
4 — 750 headwords	• All About Plants • How to Stay Healthy • Machines Then and Now • Why We Recycle	• All About Desert Life • All About Ocean Life • Animals at Night • Incredible Earth	• Animals in Art • Wonders of the Past
5 — 900 headwords	• Materials to Products • Medicine Then and Now • Transportation Then and Now • Wild Weather	• All About Islands • Animal Life Cycles • Exploring Our World • Great Migrations	• Homes Around the World • Our World in Art
6 — 1,050 headwords	• Cells and Microbes • Clothes Then and Now • Incredible Energy • Your Amazing Body	• All About Space • Caring for Our Planet • Earth Then and Now • Wonderful Ecosystems	• Food Around the World • Helping Around the World